The Kindness Givers' Formula

Four Simple Steps for Restoring Light, Hope, Love, Unity, and Peace To Our Troubled World

By

RANDALL D. MCNEELY

PRAISE FOR THE KINDNESS GIVERS' FORMULA

This sweet little book is the exact right amount and kind of information we need to restore our faith in humanity and the world. With actionable advice and great stories, this giving formula is guaranteed to put you and keep you in a positive mood!

Jordan Gross, Author
The Journey to Cloud Nine

Reading this book will inspire and give direction to anyone who wants to make a positive impact in our world. Although *The Kindness Givers' Formula* seems easy to implement, the impact of showing kindness to our fellow human beings is long lasting and profound.

This book is a must read if there's a desire in your heart to do a little more each day to brighten someone else's day! Our world needs more inspired messengers of goodness, kindness, truth and light like Randy McNeely!

Elia Gourgouris PhD, Author
7 Keys to Navigating a Crisis and
#1 Best-Selling Book
7 Paths to Lasting Happiness
President of The Happiness Center

The Kindness Givers' Formula totally resonated with me. It is a solution for our time; a formula to bring back civility and peace to a troubled world. I highly recommend it because I know you will receive more out of the kindness you give than the people for whom it is intended.

Niankoro Yeah SAMAKÉ
Strategic Advisor - Empower Mali
Former Malian Ambassador to India

The Kindness Givers' Formula is a quick read and full of great advice. Kindness can change the world, but we often struggle to look within ourselves and make the commitment to transformation. There are lots of nuggets in here to make you want to strive to do better.

Tyler Menke, Author
The Pirate's Guide to Sales

The Kindness Givers' Formula is a game changer, so needed for our time when hate and vitriol seem to be becoming the norm. The book is an easy, enjoyable, motivating read and I absolutely love the formula! It's simple, easy to implement, and it has an immediate impact for good, both on the giver and the receiver.

If you want to know how you can make a powerful difference for good, this is the book for you!

Barbara Brooks
SecondActWomen

The best endorsement I can give *The Kindness Givers' Formula* is that within an hour of reading this great book I sent out over twenty 'love notes' to people who had impacted my life and needed to know how much I appreciated them. Kindness works wonders for the soul.

James W. Ritchie
Former Senior VP Over Sales and Training
Franklin, now Franklin Covey

I love the book titled *The Kindness Givers' Formula: Four Steps for Restoring Light, Hope, Love, Unity, and Peace to Our Troubled World.*

Simple, straightforward, powerful and effective advice for establishing the habit of daily intentional kindness, a big part of the solution for restoring light, hope, love, unity, and peace to our troubled world.

Dan Nielson
Founder, Publisher, Author, Speaker and CEO
America's Healthcare Leaders

Contents

DEDICATION

To my kind-hearted sweetheart and children who inspire me to want to be the best man I can be.

In loving memory of my dear mother, Carolyn Ruth Whitaker Adams who taught me to always stop and smell the roses!

FOREWARD

I've known Randy McNeely for several years now. As I read his book about becoming a Kindness Giver, I could see him in every step of the process...it is simply how he lives. Being kind is second nature for Randy—a sixth sense. He has always been interested in being kind, doing good, and making a difference.

Likely, it is no coincidence this book is in your hands. If you believe the world is in need of a powerful yet simple formula for increasing and spreading kindness, this is the book for you. If you believe you can be a kinder person today and tomorrow than you were yesterday, and influence everyone around your circle to do the same, this is the book for you.

As you plan for a day of kindness, remember, your purposeful acts will change the world. My gratitude to Randy for making this so approachable and easy to implement.

Steven A. Hitz
Co-founder
Launching Leaders Worldwide

INTRODUCTION

Darkness cannot drive out darkness; only light can do that. Hate cannot drive out hate; only love can do that.

Martin Luther King, Jr.

In the wake of the mass shootings in Texas, Ohio, and California and the violence in so many other locations, our nation's collective soul is aching. Our hearts go out to those who have been injured, and to their families and friends, and more especially to the living who are now mourning the loss of loved ones.

Sadly, these terrible tragedies aren't the only cause for national pain. We seem to be facing a crisis of epic proportions. Just as a tidal wave erodes and displaces everything in its path, darkness, despair, hate, division and contention, so readily visible in this digital age, are eroding and displacing life sustaining light, hope, love, unity and peace. But how?

Hate and its cohorts have more avenues of entry into our lives than ever before. They are now paraded before our eyes 24x7x365 through a plethora of digital devices via the Internet, television, the news, movies, and especially on social media. Is it any wonder, with the readily accessible diet of this "downer fodder" which engenders feelings of darkness, doubt and despair, that there has been a precipitous rise in depression and suicide among young people? They've gotten so engaged in a digital world that far too many have disengaged from the real world.

The same could be said for many adults.

The question we must ask ourselves is what is to be done to stem this horrendous tide? How can we stop the exponential erosion and restore light, hope, love, unity and peace to the world? Can anything be done? Shall we leave it to the politicians to resolve? How well has that worked so far? Will we, stand around wringing our hands wondering what to do, wishing we could do something but, feeling powerless, do nothing? Of course, to take that position is to embrace complete abdication of all we owe to ourselves, our families, our posterity, our communities, our nations, and to the world.

So, again, what is to be done? Can you and I possibly make a difference? The answer is a resounding **YES,** and *The Kindness Givers' Formula, Four Simple Steps for Restoring Light, Hope, Love, Unity, and Peace* provides an easy yet powerfully effective solution. Its message is one of hope that offers a straightforward four-step-habit-building method the enables anyone who employs it to unleash the power of kindness and start having an immediate impact for good. Following the formula will touch hearts and change lives – the lives of the kindness receivers and, more especially, the lives of the Kindness Givers.

We've seen the powerful ability that kindness has to reach inside people's hearts and bring forth a desire to bless and serve others. This power is always on display after tornadoes, hurricanes, earthquakes, and floods as people from all races, political views, and varying walks of life come together, setting aside their differences to help those in need. We're all familiar with and appreciate the feelings of hope and goodwill that come as a result.

We find evidence of kindness' strength in the "Pay it Forward" movement which masterfully depicts how kindness begets kindness because kindness is contagious.

We see the power of kindness to ripple through time when we read about what has been labeled as the miraculous Christmas of 1914, when a truce was declared for one night and day on the Western Front in World War I. There the tumultuous noises of battle ceased, and British, French, Belgian, and German troops came together to celebrate, sing carols and exchange gifts. "...A century later, the truce has been remembered as a testament to the power of hope and humanity in a truly dark hour of history."[1] The kindness on display that night still echoes through the corridors of time to lift and inspire our hearts today. If ever there was a time when we needed hope and humanity in a dark hour of history, that time is now.

I invite you to develop the daily habit of being intentional Kindness Givers—kindness heroes who inspire hope, lift hearts, and bless lives. Join me in this noble cause to restore light, love, hope, unity and peace by reading on, learning and applying *The Kindness Givers' Formula*, and inviting and encouraging everyone within your sphere of influence to do the same.

"But," you might ask, "even if I implement the 'Kindness Givers' Formula', what good will it really do? Can kindness stop a bullet?"

No. Kindness can't stop a fired bullet. What kindness can do, however, is turn on the light of hope and faith in people's lives. It can soften and change hearts in such a way that it may prevent bullets from being fired in the first place. We will never know how many of the lives of malice pushers and violence perpetrators could have been changed or how many lost lives could have been saved if the pushers and perpetrators had been exposed to greater love and kindness.

You may also think, "But I'm just one person. I'm nobody special. How can my simple efforts possibly have any kind of 'transformational impact for good?'"

To that question I respond by saying, "When thoughts like these come, think of honey bees."

Why honey bees?

Honey bees are an amazing example of what collaborative cooperation can accomplish. Each individual bee is driven to fly thousands of miles to thousands of flowers to gather nectar which is then returned to the hive and condensed into sweet, delicious honey. Interestingly, each individual worker bee, over their lifespan of 6-8 weeks only produces one-twelfth of a teaspoon of honey.[2] Thinking about it, that seems like very little for so much work. Yet each bee's contribution is vital to the hive. Why? Each contribution is vital because the combined efforts of 20,000 to 60,000 bees produce from 60 to 100 pounds of honey per year,[3] which allows the hive to survive and thrive.

As with the contribution of honey bees, our "one-twelfth" actions may not seem like much taken by themselves. But over time, through the cumulative effect of thousands, hundreds of thousands, even millions of simple acts of caring, the sweet nectar of kindness can and will have a huge transformational impact on the world. As with the honey bees, our collective efforts will ensure that humanity will pull through this dark time and continue to flourish in the future!

How?

The answer is not complicated. As discussed previously kindness begets kindness because kindness is contagious. Simple acts of kindness often have a way of penetrating hearts and changing lives in ways that nothing else can.

The fomenters of hate and malice are not sitting idle. If we would turn the tide in this crisis, we must be just as engaged and active as they are!

The world needs to know that hope and humanity still exist. They need to believe that light, hope, love, unity, and peace can be restored. I firmly believe that when we unleash the full influence of committed Kindness Givers, the world will change overnight. The world needs people with the courage and determination to unleash that power in order push back against the tidal wave of hate and darkness that is striving to overwhelm us.

The opportunity is before us. Together we can do this. We can make a solid difference for good, if we will. The time to be up and taking action is now.

Are you ready?

THE KINDNESS GIVERS' FORMULA

If you have kindness in your heart, you offer acts of kindness to touch the hearts of others wherever you go—whether they are random or planned. Kindness becomes a way of life.

Roy T. Bennett

I am a big fan of the amazing servant leader, and prolific author, Dr. John Maxwell. He is well known in the leadership arena, particularly for his marvelous capability to add value and bring profitability to others. In other words, he constantly strives to lift and build those around him and is continually learning and working to improve so that the information he provides is useful (i.e. profitable) to those he serves.

In January of this year, Dr. Maxwell shared a five-step formula for daily adding value to others. He promised the audience at Christ Fellowship Church that if they would follow it, they would have the best year ever. That simple formula is this:

Every day...

1) Value people.
2) Think of things to add value to people.
3) Look for ways to add value to people.

4) Do things that add value to people.
5) Encourage others to add value to people.[4]

I love formulas like that—simple, succinct, and effective because they are easy to follow and, when followed appropriately, they can produce powerful results.

I especially appreciate that formula because in studying it, I had an "aha" moment. For months, for years really, as hate has continued to increase, I've been searching for a way to succinctly describe the soul-lifting, life-saving method of kindness giving for combating hate and its accompanying darkness.

Now, inspired by Dr. Maxwell and following his pattern, *The Kindness Givers' Formula* has taken shape. The formula is four simple, habit-building and easy-to-follow-and-implement steps.

Every day...

1) Determine to be a Kindness Giver.
2) Think of and plan ways to be a Kindness Giver.
3) Look for and act on opportunities to be a Kindness Giver.
4) Invite and encourage others to be Kindness Givers.

That's it – straightforward, and, with a little practice, easy to apply.

In speaking to his audience about the "Adding Value" formula, Dr. Maxwell promised them that if they would follow the formula, they would have the best year ever.

Like Dr. Maxwell, I'm bold enough to promise you that if you will learn and apply *The Kindness Givers' Formula*, as discussed in the following sections, you will be agents for change. You will be instruments of goodness. You will be bearers of the light, hope, love, unity and peace—Kindness Givers who inspire hope and dispel darkness. Your actions will be life transformational both for you and those you serve. You will make the rest of this year and the years following the best years of your life and have the blessing of helping others to do the same.

DETERMINE TO BE A KINDNESS GIVER

There is no chance, no destiny, no fate, that can circumvent, or hinder or control the firm resolve of a determined soul.

Ella Wheeler Wilcox

One of the greatest gifts we have as human beings, possibly the greatest gift, is the ability to choose. We are not driven like brute beasts merely to act on instinct, but we have the ability to think and reason and make conscious choices about what we will or won't do. We have the opportunity to govern our minds, notwithstanding the circumstances in which we find ourselves. That is powerful.

It is that power that we can harness every day to determine that we will be intentional Kindness Givers.

What does that take? Does it mean I just get up and say, "I'm going to be a Kindness Giver today?"

For some that might work. But for me, and I dare guess for the majority of people, it takes a little more than that. I personally find it helpful to pray. I believe in God and believe that He hears and answers my prayers. I pray daily for Him to fill me with love and help me to stay focused and firmly determined to be a Kindness Giver at all times. That's what works for me.

Prayer may work for you as well, or meditation or another method may help. Take the time to find what works best for you in accordance with your beliefs and values.

I've also found it helpful to give myself a little pep talk, to remind myself of my "Why" which drives me to do what I do. Though it might sound silly to some, I follow what I call the "Lightning McQueen" method. Remember the parts in Cars where Lightning is in the back of his semi-truck talking to himself before big races?

"Speed. I am speed. One winner. Forty-two losers. I eat losers for breakfast...Speed. Faster than Fast. Quicker than quick. I am Lightning."[5]

Instead of sitting in the back of a large semi, I sit in my office chair and think, "I am kindness. I am goodness. I was born to do great things. I was born to make a difference for good. I am a light and love restorer. I am a hate disruptor because I choose to be a Kindness Giver. I am kindness." As needed, I repeat those thoughts in my head, wherever I am.

Obviously, the words or the order might vary from day to day, but you get the picture.

We've all used similar methods before when facing what seems to be a great challenge. We do so to remind ourselves of who we are and our "Why" for doing what we're doing in order to prepare ourselves mentally and emotionally to go out and give our very best.

Every one of us is capable of putting this step into practice and putting aside any apprehension we may have if we are willing to put forth the effort. The power is in us and the world needs us.

By intentionally determining and choosing to be Kindness Givers, we intentionally choose to become emissaries of kindness who restore light, hope, love, unity and peace; we intentionally choose to make a difference in the lives of others; we intentionally choose to have a transformational impact for good on the world.

THINK OF AND PLAN FOR WAYS TO BE A KINDNESS GIVER

Kindness is a vast color that only your heart knows how to paint.

RAKtivist

Plutarch, an ancient Greek philosopher, once said "the mind is not a vessel to be filled, but a fire to be kindled."[6]

In relation to kindness giving, the question becomes, "What can we do to kindle our mind's fire with thoughts of ways to give kindness?"

A simple approach that I follow is to take a few minutes every day, early in the morning, and find a quiet space to review my day. I am fortunate enough to have an office where I can seclude myself and take the time to ponder.

Once settled in my chair, I think about what I will be doing, where I will be going, and who I will be with during the day. Then I think about and plan out in my mind potential acts of kindness I can do.

I first think of potential ways to show kindness at home before leaving for work – a hug and kiss for my wife and kids, a made bed, a note of affection. Then I think of things I might do outside the home, in my neighborhood when I'm walking for exercise, on my way to work, at work and on my way home. What are the ways I can show kindness in each situation? I can call a friendly greeting, say "Hi", smile, pick up trash as I walk, drive courteously going to and from work, lend a listening ear while at work, and so forth. Finally, I think of what I might do in the evening when I'm back home. I plan out all of these things in my head and store them there.

That's what works for me. However, each person's situation and circumstances are different. Not everyone has an office. Where I take the time to review and plan potential possibilities out in my head, that may not work for everyone. Take the time to assess your own situation and determine what will work best for you.

Ideas for giving kindness abound! If we're mindful, and take the time to ponder, we won't have any problem kindling our kindness fire. With that fire burning brightly, we are ready for the next step.

LOOK FOR AND ACT ON OPPORTUNITIES TO BE A KINDNESS GIVER

A single act of kindness throws out roots in all directions and the roots spring up and make new trees.

Amelia Earhart

With your determination to be a Kindness Giver set, and your thoughts and plans laid for potential acts of kindness, the moment of truth has come. The time to look for and act on opportunities to be a Kindness Giver has arrived.

Here are a few things to keep in mind as you go forth to be Kindness Givers.

First, it is important to remember my use of the word "potential" in describing thinking and planning. I use "potential" because plans don't always go as expected. We can't predict what we will or won't encounter, even at home. Some situations we expect to find may not materialize and opportunities that weren't considered may very well present themselves. Be prepared to be flexible. Be prepared to look anywhere and everywhere. You never know what you will find or where you will find it.

Second, start with simple things and work up from there according to your time, opportunities, and capacity. A simple thank you (i.e. gratitude) is an act of kindness. A smile is an act of kindness. Holding the door for someone is an act of kindness. Being cheerful is an act of kindness. A compliment or a word of encouragement or praise is an act of kindness. Remember simple actions and simple words have great power. Not only can they affect people in the moment, but they can continue reverberating through time for decades, centuries, and even millennia.

For instance, an experience in my life thirty-five years ago still echoes in my heart and stirs strong emotion. I feel that stirring now even as I'm typing this.

As a teenager my family was in great turmoil and my self-esteem was nearly non-existent. Then one day nine simple words penetrated my soul and changed my life forever. In preparation for a student council meeting, I had just passed out an agenda that I had personally typed. A friend, one of the most popular and prettiest girls in the school (the kind a guy wants to talk to but can't because his tongue feels three feet thick), came in just at that moment, picked up a copy of the agenda and started reading through it. After looking at it for a few seconds, she pointed out to me, not in an unkind way, that I had misspelled the word "miscellaneous." Feeling utterly humiliated and embarrassed, I responded, "Oh! I guess you think I'm pretty stupid, huh."

Then came the words that I've never forgotten.

"Oh, no I don't. I think you're pretty neat!"

I can't begin to describe in words how I felt in that moment. I didn't realize at the time how much I needed to hear someone, anyone, point out to me that I had value and that I was "pretty neat!" I turned, quickly left the room, then ran to the bathroom and locked myself in a stall because I didn't want anyone to see me crying.

To this day every time I think of that experience, I get choked up and thank God for my friend's kindness to me. Her kindness not only blessed me, but it has been the driving force, in many ways, behind my desire to lift, serve, and bless others throughout my life. It is a driving force behind my writing this book.

Remember, simple words and actions can have great power.

Third, when an opportunity to give kindness presents itself, if you're able to do something, act on it. Don't wait, or it may pass you by. You don't know when your words or actions may touch someone's life as my friend's words touched mine.

Another personal experience serves as an illustration.

I travel a lot and I was staying at a hotel, I believe in Louisiana, though I don't recall for sure now. As I was walking down the hall, a lady from the hotel cleaning crew was walking toward me. As she got closer, I had the feeling I should tell her how much I appreciated all the effort she and other cleaning staff members put into making my stay at the hotel comfortable. I almost ignored the feeling, but then, as she was about to pass by me, I spoke up and thanked her. It wasn't that big of a thing for me to do and the words were not hard to say. But the look on her face was priceless. She got emotional and thanked me profusely for my compliment. What she said next left me flabbergasted.

"In the four years I've worked here, you are the first person that has ever thanked me for my work. Thank you. Thank you ever so much. You've made my day!"

How glad I am that I followed my feelings!

Fourth, if you find yourself in a situation like the one I've just described, and you feel intimidated at the thought of talking to a complete stranger, you're not alone. Talking to strangers is a definite non-comfort zone situation for many people. Trust me, I've been there. Even though I'm an extrovert and generally have no problem talking to strangers, I still sometimes get really nervous for reasons I don't understand. Why do you think I hesitated and almost let that cleaning lady pass by without saying anything?

But, just as I did, you can overcome your fear. What did I do? For me, I remembered my "Why" and forced myself to open my mouth and speak. The fact that I've repeated to myself over and over again the mantra that "I make a difference for good," gives me the strength to stifle my fears and speak out. That's what works for me. You might try the same thing or find another method. Find a way that works best for you to help you have the courage to step out of your comfort zone and speak up. You can do it!

Fifth, and closely tied to the fourth suggestion above, **always** assume the best in others. Being human, as hard as we strive not to, more often than not we judge others by their appearance, by their accent, ethnicity, race, sexual orientation, wealth or poverty. It is those judgements, uncontrolled, that lead, in great measure, to the issues with hate we are currently experiencing. To succeed as Kindness Givers, however, we must always strive to remember that none of those things matter. When it comes to giving kindness, remember, we are all human beings, and kindness knows no barriers. As you cast the bread of kindness in love to others, it will always come back multiplied. **Always, always, always** assume the best in others.

Sixth, remember that practice makes perfect. You might feel like it is not in your nature to give kindness, yet as you practice, as you take simple steps and work up from there, you can and will change. Abraham Lincoln is credited with saying, "Most folks are about as happy as they make up their minds to be."[7] That phrase could easily be changed to, "Most folks are as kind as they make up their minds to be." As with golf or piano playing or any other talent that takes practice to continually improve, the more you practice giving kindness, the more natural it will become and the easier it will be.

Finally, there will be times, no matter how good your intentions, when some people will not accept your kind gestures or actions. It happens from time to time but very rarely. At those times, be patient, don't let yourself get discouraged, and move on. None of us can control how others will react. We can only control how we act.

INVITE AND ENCOURAGE OTHERS TO BE KINDNESS GIVERS

I can do things you cannot, you can do things I cannot; together we can do great things.

Mother Teresa

A natural consequence of both giving and receiving genuine kindness is feelings of gratitude that fill our hearts and the natural lightening of our own burdens and personal challenges. There is something divine about those feelings and when they come, we are so thankful that we can't help but want to turn around and give love and kindness away. The more we do, the more we experience such amazing feelings of happiness and well-being inside that we want to do it again, and again, and again. It becomes addicting!

As you put the first three steps of *The Kindness Givers' Formula* into practice, I can promise you that the feelings described above will start to come. However, the process isn't complete. If you want to experience the described feelings to the fullest extent, to take those feelings to the "next level," then you will need to implement the final step. You will need to invite and encourage others to be Kindness Givers. Considered another way, you will need to become Kindness Recruiters.

Why?

There are two reasons for becoming Kindness Recruiters.

The first reason is love for family and friends. Once you start experiencing the feelings of gratitude, thankfulness, happiness and joy that come from giving kindness, you will naturally want to invite those you care about to do the same thing so they can experience those feelings themselves.

The second reason is love for our neighbors, our community, our nation, and the world. As has been shown and as we naturally understand, unleashing kindness is the most effective way to restore the light, hope, love, unity and peace that dispel hate and all of its derivatives. Hate pushers are continually recruiting new members to their ranks. To effectively counter their activities and win this battle, we must do the same. We must do everything we can to fill our neighborhoods, our communities, our nations, and the world with love and kindness.

"But how? Do I need to write a book, go on a speaking tour, start a blog or start a kindness giving organization?"

All of those things would be awesome, and if you're in a position to do so, go for it!

However, most people are not in that position. "Okay, then what do you suggest?"

The answer is pretty simple really.

First, work within your sphere of influence. Light the way for others by being an example of kindness wherever you go. Others will see your example, notice how happy and cheerful you are and wonder why. When they ask you, tell them and invite them to do the same thing. Some may not wish to, but many will.

Second, as your time and capacity permits, work to expand your sphere of influence. For me, that means blogging, book writing, joining social media groups and making posts about kindness and through them inviting and encouraging others to be kind. For you it might mean the same thing or something different. Start where you are, determine what you can do in your current circumstances, and work up from there. If your current circumstances don't work for you, look for ways to change them.

That's it.

"But," you might say, "I'm a nobody. I can't light the way for anyone. Why would anyone pay attention to me?"

No one is a nobody. No matter who you are, no matter where you're from, no matter what your race or gender may be, everyone is a somebody who has the capacity and capability to be a kind body! Unlike sports where you have to prove over and over again that you have the "right stuff" to be chosen for an "All Star" team, everyone who chooses to give kindness becomes a "Kindness All Star" the moment they take action!

You can do it! As you put forth the effort and do simple acts of kindness, people will notice, and the majority will be grateful and will want to emulate your actions.

If you still doubt yourself, remember honey bees and the cumulative power of multiple individual actions when considered together. Remember that kindness begets kindness because kindness is contagious—think "Pay it Forward."

KINDNESS IN ACTION – SIMPLE EXAMPLES OF GIVING AND RECEIVING KINDNESS

Too often we underestimate the power of a touch, a smile, a kind word, a listening ear, an honest compliment, or the smallest act of caring, all of which have the potential to turn a life around.

Leo Buscaglia

The following short stories are true experiences from my own life as well as the life of my dear friend, Christopher M. "Chris" Jones. Chris is the author of the beloved Facebook blog, Mitchell's Journey which catalogues Chris's and his family's experiences with their son Mitchell, both during Mitchell's battle with Duchenne muscular dystrophy and following his passing. Chris, who epitomizes what it means to be a Kindness Giver, has graciously consented to allow me to share a few of his personal experiences with receiving kindness because they, along with my life experiences, serve as examples of the powerful effect of kindness in action.

None of these stories are shared with a spirit of self-aggrandizement, but rather in the spirit of hope that they will inspire you, the reader, with your own ideas for spreading kindness.

NOTE: In my personal stories, the names of friends or neighbors have been changed. In Chris's stories, the names are the same as they appear on his Facebook blog. Additionally, Chris's stories have had minor edits to accommodate the format of this book.

RANDY - AT THE AIRPORT

Because I travel a lot as a consultant, I build up a lot of frequent flyer miles with various airlines. On one occasion I was traveling with American Airlines (AA) as a "Gold" member and had enough miles to get an upgrade to First Class. I was excited as I anticipated how comfortable and roomy the flight home would be.

While waiting for my flight, I saw an older man with a knee brace and crutches hobble to a seat and set himself down. I don't recall who started it, but I ended up having a conversation in which the man, whom I'll call Dan, explained that he had just had a knee replacement. I asked him where he was sitting for the flight. "In the economy section," was his reply. Dan was not a small man. Anyone who has ridden in the economy section of any airline knows that having a big, tall man try to sit there comfortably is like trying to stuff a five-pound trout into a sardine can and expecting it to fit. It won't work. So, after talking with my new friend for a few minutes, I decided to see if I could switch places with him. It took some negotiating with the airline, but the arrangements were soon made. The only catch was that we would have to wait to make the switch until everyone had boarded. Once the boarding was completed, including Dan getting on and squeezing into the economy section, the stewardess went back and helped Dan come up front. She stowed his crutches and he was able to sit in the very front seat that had extra leg room. His gratitude was boundless. My heart was also bursting with gratitude at seeing his joy and knowing that I had been fortunate enough to be in a position to give kindness to a fellow passenger.

My ride in the economy section was extra comfy that day. The closeness of the seats didn't magically change. Rather, those warm feelings of gratitude stayed with me the whole flight home and so occupied my mind that I didn't have time to think about any bodily discomfort. Those feelings of warmth re-ignite in my heart whenever I think about that experience.

CHRIS – THE BETTER WAY[8]

On Mitchell's last trip to work with me a colleague went out of his way to talk to Mitch and make him feel important. When I think back on this moment my heart is filled with gratitude because there were probably a million-and-one reasons he could have ignored Mitch and focused only on the tasks that weighted heavy on his shoulders. I suppose, if he were like many people today swept up in the rush and flurry of things, he might have felt bothered, slowed down or flustered because there was a kid in the office. That was not how Corey treated my son, for he chose the better way. This moment reminded me of something William Phelps said, "The first test of a gentleman: his respect for those who can be of no possible value to him." I have always loved that observation and I saw it in action that day.

Corey, understanding the true value of a soul, knew there was more to life than work and took time to love my son. If Mitch had lived a full life, I am sure he would have remembered that exchange with Corey as one of those building moments ... those rare exchanges when you're young that make you feel special and important and change you a little on the inside.

When we left work, Mitch said in his quiet voice, "Dad, that man was really nice to me. Is everyone you work with that nice?" Immediately I felt a lump in my throat because I knew how much little Mitch valued kindness ... and he was given the gift of kindness by Corey. I told him, "I think so, Mitchie. I surely hope so."

Fast forward a few months and I found myself at my little boy's funeral, devastated and bewildered with grief. We had just said our final goodbyes and closed the casket and began the impossible walk down the hall to the chapel. My knees almost gave out a couple of times because my body just wanted to fall to the ground and weep.

As we began to turn the corner, I saw Corey walking into the building to offer his love and support. He lived so far away from us and probably had a million-and-one reasons to not go, but he made it a point to offer love and kindness to our family. I quickly broke formation and gave him a hug just before we entered the chapel. Suddenly, in my mind, I heard Mitchell's voice, almost like a whisper, "Dad, that man was really nice to me." In my heart I said to my son, "Mitch, you were right, that man IS really nice ... and nothing else matters." He doesn't know this, but Corey's gift of kindness to Mitch was also a gift to me because he gave my boy the gift of time and attention and made him happy. He truly showed us that kindness is always the better way.

RANDY- MR. SMILEY

When I was in college, I worked as a custodian from 4AM to 8AM – not the most glamorous work schedule on the planet. As early as it was, I determined to do my best to be cheerful. Whenever anyone passed by, I made it a point to greet them with a smile and say "Hi". Over time I became known as Mr. Smiley.

One morning I was sweeping in front of the student center and noticed a lady coming up the walk to the entrance. I don't remember what her outfit looked like, but I remember smiling, saying "Hi", and telling her she looked nice that day. Then I continued sweeping, not thinking anything more about it.

A couple of hours later, as I was leaving, I checked my assigned cubby hole to see if there were any notes from my boss with instructions for the next day. There were no notes, but, to my surprise, there was a blue envelope. I opened the envelope and it contained a note and ten bookstore bucks. The note said something like, "Thank you for your smile and kind words this morning. As I walked in, I was feeling pretty lousy about myself. Your smile and compliment drove those feelings away. You made my day! Enjoy the bookstore bucks."

I repacked the envelope and headed to my early morning class, seemingly lighter on my feet and filled with happiness that I had been able to lift someone's heart.

CHRIS – A SUPERNAL GIFT (Original Title – So Empty, Yet So Full)[9]

It was an especially hot summer day when two mothers and 4 children walked into Pioneer Park, each with an arm full of gifts they were about to give away. Quietly they began placing all manner of toys throughout the playground. Each toy had a sticker attached to it with an invitation to play with and keep, signed Mitchell's Journey.

Cathy O'Grady, a follower-turned-friend from Boston, was in Salt Lake City and wanted to do something in memory of little Mitch. So, she purchased two carts of toys that included baseball bats, footballs, bubbles, chalk, soccer balls and other things kids used to play with before the advent of technology ... before the age of digital isolation and endless distraction.

She was kind enough to let me follow her and a friend, Tracey Langston, so I could take photos of their random act of love and kindness in memory of Mitch. Each of them wore a Miles for Mitchell shirt because they wanted to take my son with them.

"Watch how parents will put their phones down and suddenly start playing with their children when they're given a toy." Cathy said. Sure enough, exactly as she described, I saw it with my own eyes. Parents who moments earlier were busy scrolling through never ending streams of Pinterest posts, social feeds, texts, emails and other things suddenly set their devices down and began to play with their children.

I saw adorable little kids stumble into a lonely soccer ball, pick it up with curiosity and then show it to their parents as though they won a lottery. I marveled at how these small, inexpensive toys changed how people interacted with one another. As these anonymous gifts were discovered, the playground went from friendly to an excited frolic.

After these good Samaritans were done placing toys ... when parents and children alike were playing with one another, I told Cathy how humbled I was by her act of kindness. As my eyes filled with tears ... fighting back a wave of grief ... I told Cathy something about little Mitch just before he passed away. As Mitch was facing the realities of his own death he wept and wept as he told me how much he wished he could be like regular kids. My soul unraveled and my heart fell to the floor as I heard my son describe what he wanted to do in "real life" but could not. "Dad, I don't want to ride a skate board in a video game, I want to do it for reals." Mitch sobbed in ways only a dying child can know. And my soul writhed.

I told Cathy how grateful I was for the gifts she gave others. She didn't just give toys, you see. These little gifts were a means to a much greater end. Cathy gave the gift of play. The gift of relationships.

I am so grateful for people like Cathy and Tracey ... who seek to build others up and serve with love. I wonder how the world would change if everyone gave freely and not want anything in exchange. Something divine happens when we love and lift ... for the very act of giving is itself a supernal gift.

RANDY – A CHANGE OF HEART

Mark and Christy Young were real grouches, or so it seemed to me when I first met them and for a while thereafter. As a kid, I liked to whistle and sing and did so pretty much everywhere I went. It often brought me a sense of comfort in circumstances which weren't always ideal. For some reason this always seemed to get on Mark's and Christy's nerves and if they were ever outside they would yell at me and tell me to shut up.

Over time the enmity between us escalated. Mark liked to work on his car in their driveway and blast out "raucous" music through his boom box. Whenever he did, I'd go and get my brother's boom box and put it in our tiled bathroom that acted like a massive echo chamber. I would then throw open the window and blast out Chinese opera. Needless to say, our friendliness toward each other did not increase.

That all changed, however, on a cold winter's day a few months later with one simple act. It had snowed nearly a foot of wet, heavy snow. I had just finished shoveling our front walk when I noticed Christy struggling to get her walk and driveway shoveled. Without saying anything, I walked over and helped her complete the walk, the path to their door, their front steps and porch, and the driveway.

As we worked together, any enmity there had been between Christy and I completely melted away. Later that day, I happened to overhear Christy telling Mark how I'd helped. Soon after, Mark came to our home and asked to see me. When I came to the door, he extended his hand and I nervously took it. He then thanked me for helping Christy and sincerely apologized for all the times he'd yelled at me or played his music so loud. I too apologized for being so noisy and for blasting the Chinese opera. We then said our goodbyes and he departed.

From that day on we were friends. No more yelling or blasting loud music. We were friends, and true neighbors whose hearts and lives were changed through a simple act of kindness.

CHRIS – I'VE GOT YOUR BACK[10]

In 2015 I received a message from an active military officer who said he and some colleagues would be running in honor of our son Mitch while deployed in Iraq. He offered his well wishes, prayers and love from "the dustiest place on earth."

He then concluded his letter with the following salutation:

CW3 Officer Leach
US ARMY
Blackhawk pilot

I was so moved that someone occupied with other matters would take time out of his life to remember little Mitch and support our desire to help and encourage others. I then responded to his message with the following:

[Officer Leach,]

Holy cow. That would have blown Mitchell's mind. He always admired military officers and their sacrifices to keep him safe. When he was home on hospice, he cried tears of gratitude when he received messages and photos from every branch of the military. Your doing this will be especially amazing for our family.

Thank you, good sir. On so many levels, thank you.

UT, Chris Jones
Ordinary Dad
Grateful Human

... and that was my letter to him. I had no credentials to point to, no rank or military file. The only title I held was that of ordinary dad and grateful human. I just wanted him to know how much I appreciated his gesture. In so many ways, it felt as if he was saying, "I've got your back." Although he was way over there, on the other side of the earth, he seemed to care about what was going on over here.

Then, as promised, this good officer (and father himself) sent me some photos of little

Mitch with him and in the window of his Blackhawk and indicated they'd be flying Mitch with them that day.

To think that a stranger could be so kind and thoughtful to do something like that in honor of a little boy who died, and a father who misses him deeply, humbles me.

CONCLUSION

Have I done any good in the world today?
Have I helped anyone in need?
Have I cheered up the sad and made someone
feel glad?
If not, I have failed indeed.
Has anyone's burden been lighter today
Because I was willing to share?
Have the sick and the weary been helped on
their way?
When they needed my help was I there?

There are chances for work all around just now,
Opportunities right in our way.
Do not let them pass by, saying, "Sometime I'll
try,"
But go and do something today.
'Tis noble of man to work and to give;
Love's labor has merit alone.
Only he who does something helps others to live.
To God each good work will be known.

Will L. Thompson

Now we've arrived at the conclusion of this short
work.

Here are the major takeaways!

1) Light, hope, love, unity and peace are being
eroded and displaced at an exponential rate by

darkness, despair, hate, division and contention.

2) The four simple steps of *The Kindness Givers' Formula* provide an easy yet powerfully effective solution for restoring light, hope, love, unity, and peace.

3) We can ingrain the habit of daily kindness giving into our lives by following the four simple steps of the formula every day.

Every day...

    a. Determine to be a Kindness Giver.
    b. Think of and plan ways to be a Kindness Giver.
    c. Look for and act on opportunities to be a Kindness Giver.
    d. Invite and encourage others to be Kindness Givers.

4) As we implement the steps we will reap the following benefits:

    a. We will bless the lives of all those to whom we show kindness.
    b. We will experience greater feelings of happiness and hope.
    c. The boomerang effect (what comes around goes around) will be readily apparent in our own lives as the burdens we carry and challenges we may be facing seem less daunting.

d. We will have an impact for good on everyone within our sphere of influence and the effects will ripple out from there.

5) Light, love, unity, and peace will be restored in greater abundance and our neighborhoods, communities, nations, and the world will be a much better, happier place to live.

Does *The Kindness Givers' Formula* resonate with you? If so, I invite you to come and join in this worthy cause which is worldwide in its circumference. Come and be part of a powerful movement to transform the world for good by restoring light, hope, love, unity and peace through the daily habit of intentional kindness giving. Come, stand up and be counted among a worldwide group of all-star Kindness Givers— kindness heroes who touch hearts and change lives! Come, join us, and invite and inspire others to do the same.

The task may seem daunting, especially since hate is in your face everywhere every day and nearly always upstages other, more newsworthy, items. Kindness, generally, works in the background. Hate is like chicken pox or the flu virus with symptoms readily apparent in its victims. Kindness is like our antibodies working behind the scenes, shutting down the pathogens. Hate appears to be all powerful, yet there is no hate that, over time, love and kindness cannot conquer.

As stated previously, I'm bold enough to promise you that if you will learn and apply *The Kindness Givers' Formula*, you will become agents for change. You will be instruments of goodness. You will become bearers of the light of love and kindness who inspire hope and dispel darkness. Your actions will be life transformational, both for you and those you serve. You will make the rest of this year and the years following the best years of your life and have the blessing of helping others to do the same.

The fomenters of hate and malice are not sitting idle. If we would turn the tide in this crisis, we must be just as engaged and active as they are!

Our neighborhoods, communities, nations and the entire world need to know that hope and humanity still exist. They need to believe that light, hope, love, unity and peace can be restored. The opportunity to show them is before us. Together we can do this. We can make a solid difference for good, if we will. The time to be up and taking action is now.

ACKNOWLEDGEMENTS

I would be remiss if I didn't take a few moments to acknowledge those who've been instrumental in helping me to bring this work to fruition.

First and foremost, I want thank God, my Heavenly Father, the ultimate Kindness Giver. Without His grace and kindness to me, I never could have written this work in the first place.

Second, I want to thank my lovely wife, whose editing and feedback were invaluable. How grateful I am for her and our children for their unending encouragement and support.

Third, I wish to thank Chris Jones for his kindness in allowing me to use his heart-and-soul-touching stories which represent kindness in action so well. Their conveyance of genuine love added a richness to the "Kindness in Action" chapter that would not have been there otherwise. Thank you, Chris.

Finally, thank you to all of my friends, who took the time to proofread my manuscript, offer thoughtful feedback and suggestions, and aid in the editing process. The list is too numerous to name you all, but you know who you are and to you I give a humble and heartfelt thank you.

QUOTE SOURCES

Bennett, Roy T.
https://goodreads.com/quotes/7454857-
if-you-have-kindness-in-your-heart-you-
offer-acts
[accessed 8/15/19]

Buscaglia, Leo.
https://www.brainyquote.com/quotes/leo
_buscaglia_106299
[accessed 8/15/19]

Earhart, Amelia.
https://www.passiton.com/inspirational-
quotes/7491-a-single-act-of-kindness-
throws-out-roots-in
[accessed 8/15/19]

Hall, Ron.
https://www.brainyquote.com/quotes/ro
n_hall_898977
[accessed 8/15/19]

King, Martin Luther, Jr.
https://www.brainyquote.com/quotes/ma
rtin_luther_king_jr_101472?src=t_light
[accessed 8/15/19]

RAKtivist.
https://www.randomactsofkindness.org/
kindness-quotes/271-kindness-is-a-vast-
color

[accessed 8/15/19]

Teresa, Mother.
https://www.goodreads.com/quotes/6316
8-i-can-do-things-you-cannot-you-can-do-
things
[accessed 8/15/19]

Thompson, Will L.
https://www.churchofjesuschrist.org/mu
sic/library/hymns/have-i-done-any-
good?lang=eng&_r=1
[accessed 8/15/19]

Wilcox, Ella Wheeler.
https://www.brainyquote.com/quotes/ell
a_wheeler_wilcox_121936
[accessed 8/15/19]

Wirthlin, Joseph B. (Cover Quote)
https://quizlet.com/90728402/the-virtue-
of-kindness-joseph-b-wirthlin-flash-
cards/
[accessed 9/29/19]

ENDNOTES

[1] Naina Bajekal, Silent Night, The story of The World War I Christmas Truce of 2014, 8 August 2019,
https://time.com/3643889/christmas-truce-1914/

[2] Devon Rowley, 101 Fun BEE Facts About Bees and Beekeeping, 7 August 2019,
https://www.beepods.com/101-fun-bee-facts-about-bees-and-beekeeping/

[3] Ibid.

[4] Christ Fellowship Church, YouTube, How to Have Your Best Year Ever | Dr. John Maxwell, 7 August 2019,
https://youtu.be/cxE7DCWjOvs

[5] TechWizard Gadget Reviews – Youtube – CARS – Lightning McQueen I am Speed HD, 7 August 2019,
https://www.youtube.com/watch?v=Tj9q4ADVrL4

[6] Plutarch, Brainy Quote, Plutarch Quotes, 7 August 2019,
https://www.brainyquote.com/quotes/plutarch_161334

[7] Abraham Lincoln, Good Reads, Abraham Lincoln, Quotes, Quotable Quote, 28 August 2019,
https://www.goodreads.com/quotes/5445 79-most-folks-are-about-as-happy-as-they-make-up

[8] Christopher M. Jones, The Better Way, 15 August 2019,
https://mitchellsjourney.org/essays/2014 /10/8/the-better-way?rq=kindness

[9] Christopher M. Jones, So Empty, Yet So Full, 15 August 2019,
https://mitchellsjourney.org/essays/2015 /8/20/so-empty-yet-so-full?rq=kindness

[10] Christopher M. Jones, I've Got Your Back, 15 August 2019,
https://mitchellsjourney.org/essays/2015 /4/28/ive-got-your-back?rq=KINDNESS

ABOUT THE AUTHOR

Randall D. McNeely, "Randy" is a kindness giver at heart. He is passionate about and driven to share kindness as a way of giving back for the heart touching, life changing kindness shown to him throughout his life, especially during some very difficult family challenges.

To that end Randy recently Founded Kindness Hunters International (KHI). KHI is dedicated to seeking out and sharing the stories of and raising funds for amazing kindness givers who have experienced tremendous challenges in their lives. Rather than allowing their challenges to crush them, they have used them as stepping stones of inspiration to create organizations that lift and bless the lives of others.

In addition to being an author, Randy is also a singer/songwriter and has written several patriotic songs, children's songs, and multiple religious hymns. He and his daughters recorded and released the song *Everybody Speaks Smile* to remind everyone that the simple act of sharing a genuine smile is an act of kindness that all people can understand no matter what language they speak.

Randy is married to the amazing Kimberly McNeely. They are blessed to be the parents of five children—four daughters and one son.

Contact Randy by Visiting
www.randymcneely.com